State Songs of America

State Songs of America

Edited by
M. J. Bristow

GREENWOOD PRESS
Westport, Connecticut • London

ISBN: 0–313–29298–1

First published in 2000

Greenwood Press, 88 Post Road West, Westport, CT 06881
An imprint of Greenwood Publishing Group, Inc.
www.greenwood.com

Printed in the United States of America

10 9 8 7 6 5 4 3 2 1

Copyright Acknowledgments

State; Wyoming state seal reprinted with permission from the Wyoming Office of the Secretary of State; Wyoming state song, "Wyoming March Song," reprinted with permission from Margo Bean, Casper, Wyoming.

Every reasonable effort has been made to trace the owners of copyright materials in this book, but in some instances this has proven impossible. The author and publisher will be glad to receive information leading to more complete acknowledgments in subsequent printings of the book and in the meantime extend their apologies for any omissions.

CONTENTS

Preface   *ix*
United States of America   The Star-Spangled Banner   1
Alabama   Alabama   4
Alaska   Alaska's Flag   6
Arizona   Arizona March Song   9
Arkansas   Arkansas   13
California   I Love You, California   16
Colorado   Where The Columbines Grow   20
Connecticut   Yankee Doodle   24
Delaware   Our Delaware   26
Florida   Old Folks At Home   29
Georgia   Georgia On My Mind   32
Hawaii   Hawaii Ponoi   36
Idaho   Here We Have Idaho   38
Illinois   Illinois   41
Indiana   On The Banks Of The Wabash, Far Away   43
Iowa   The Song Of Iowa   47
Kansas   Home On The Range   49
Kentucky   My Old Kentucky Home   53
Louisiana   Give Me Louisiana   56
Maine   State Of Maine Song   59
Maryland   Maryland, My Maryland!   64
Massachusetts   All Hail To Massachusetts   67
Michigan   Michigan, My Michigan   70
Minnesota   Hail! Minnesota   72
Mississippi   Go, Mississippi   74
Missouri   Missouri Waltz   77
Montana   Montana   85
Nebraska   Beautiful Nebraska   89
Nevada   Home Means Nevada   92
New Hampshire   Old New Hampshire   96
New Jersey   I'm From New Jersey   99
New Mexico   O, Fair New Mexico   103
New York   I Love New York   107
North Carolina   The Old North State   112
North Dakota   North Dakota Hymn   115
Ohio   Beautiful Ohio   117
Oklahoma   Oklahoma   120
Oregon   Oregon, My Oregon   125
Pennsylvania   Pennsylvania   127
Rhode Island   Rhode Island   130
South Carolina   Carolina   133
South Dakota   Hail! South Dakota   135
Tennessee   Rocky Top   138
Texas   Texas, Our Texas   141
Utah   Utah, We Love Thee   144
Vermont   Hail, Vermont!   146
Virginia   Carry Me Back To Old Virginny   149
Washington   Washington My Home   150

West Virginia	The West Virginia Hills	154
Wisconsin	On, Wisconsin!	157
Wyoming	Wyoming March Song	159
Appendix		*163*
Composers		*165*
Lyricists		*167*
Titles		*169*

PREFACE

This collection, *State Songs of America*, provides music and lyrics for the official songs adopted by state governments. It includes the national anthem and songs for all of the states except Virginia, which does not have an official state song at the present time. The songs are arranged alphabetically by state. Each song has a single vocal line over a piano accompaniment, with one verse only under the vocal line and remaining verses appearing separately. In most cases the version of the melody and the accompaniment is that officially authorized by the state. Each entry includes the date that the state adopted the song. Some entries include brief footnotes giving the history of the song.

The entries also include a facsimile of the state seal or the state arms above the song. It is hoped that this collection will be a useful reference book for those wanting to perform a state song or to find the songs of other states.

The editor would like to acknowledge the valuable contributions of all those who have generously assisted in the development of this project. Special thanks are due to Dr. William Leonard Reed of London, England; the late Dr. Thomas Marshall Cartledge of Denver, Colorado; Rob Wallace of Grand Junction, Colorado and the late Mrs. Helen Davis of South Bend, Washington (the author and composer of the Washington state song). Gratitude is also extended to the various Governors and Secretaries of State who have graciously given permission for the use of their state song and state seal and to other official bodies for their cooperation.

Some of the footnotes contain quotations from Benjamin F. Shearer and Barbara S. Shearer, *State Names, Seals, Flags, and Symbols: A Historical Guide, Revised and Expanded* (Greenwood Press, 1994, pp. 197–208).

UNITED STATES OF AMERICA
The Star-Spangled Banner

Words by
FRANCIS SCOTT KEY (1779-1843)

Composer unknown*

Maestoso

1. O—— say, can you see, by the dawn's ear - ly light, What so proud - ly we hailed at the twi - light's last gleam - ing, Whose broad

stripes and bright stars, through the pe - ril - ous fight, O'er the ram - parts we watched were so gal - lant - ly stream - ing? And the

Words and music officially designated as the National Anthem by Act of Congress approved by the President, 3 March, 1931.
* The English composer John Stafford Smith (c. 1750-1836) in his fifth collection of glees (1799) published an arrangement of 'To Anacreon in Heaven,' the tune to which Francis Scott Key later wrote 'The Star-Spangled Banner.' This has led to his being mistakenly regarded as the composer of the tune, whose actual origin is unknown.

land_____ of the free and the home of the brave?

2. On the shore, dimly seen through the mists of the deep,
   Where the foe's haughty host in dread silence reposes,
   What is that which the breeze, o'er the towering steep,
   As it fitfully blows, half conceals, half discloses?
   Now it catches the gleam of the morning's first beam,
   In full glory reflected now shines on the stream;
   'Tis the Star-Spangled Banner, O long may it wave
   O'er the land of the free and the home of the brave!

3. O thus be it ever when free man shall stand
   Between their loved homes and the war's desolation!
   Blest with victory and peace, may the heaven-rescued land
   Praise the Power that hath made and preserved us a nation.
   Then conquer we must, for our cause it is just,
   And this be our motto: 'In God is our trust.'
   And the Star-Spangled Banner in triumph shall wave
   O'er the land of the free and the home of the brave.

ALABAMA
Alabama

Words by
JULIA STRUDWICK TUTWILER (1841-1916)

Music by
EDNA GOCKEL GUSSEN (1878-1937)

1. Al - a-bam- a, Al - a-bam- a, We will aye be true to thee,

From thy South- ern shores where grow - eth By the_ sea thy o - range tree.

To_ thy North- ern vale where flow - eth Deep and blue thy Ten- nes- see,

Officially adopted on 9 March 1931.
By the time the legislature officially adopted the song, it had already been in use for ten years as the State Song.
In 1917, the Alabama Federation of Music Clubs endorsed the song and gave it an award at its annual convention.

Al - a-bam-a, Al - a-bam-a, We will— aye be true to thee!

2. Broad the Stream whose name thou bearest;
   Grand thy Bigbee rolls along;
   Fair thy Coosa–Tallapoosa,
   Bold thy Warrior, dark and strong,
   Goodlier than the land that Moses
   Climbed lone Nebo's Mount to see,
   Alabama, Alabama,
   We will aye be true to thee!

3. From thy prairies broad and fertile,
   Where thy snow-white cotton shines,
   To the hills where coal and iron
   Hide in thy exhaustless mines,
   Strong-armed miners–sturdy farmers;
   Loyal hearts whate'er we be,
   Alabama, Alabama,
   We will aye be true to thee!

4. From thy quarries where the marble
   White as that of Paros gleams,
   Waiting till thy sculptor's chisel
   Wake to life thy poet's dreams;
   For not only wealth of nature,
   Wealth of mind hast thou to fee,
   Alabama, Alabama,
   We will aye be true to thee!

5. Where the perfumed south-wind whispers
   Thy magnolia groves among,
   Softer than a mother's kisses,
   Sweeter than a mother's song;
   Where the golden jasmine trailing
   Woos the treasure-laden bee,
   Alabama, Alabama,
   We will aye be true to thee!

6. Brave and pure thy men and women,
   Better this than corn and wine.
   Make us worthy, God in Heaven,
   Of this goodly land of Thine;
   Hearts as open as our doorways,.
   Liberal hands and spirits free,
   Alabama, Alabama,
   We will aye be true to thee!

7. Little, little can I give thee,
   Alabama, mother mine;
   But that little– hand, brain, spirit,
   All I have and am are thine.
   Take, O take the gift and giver,
   Take and serve thyself with me,
   Alabama, Alabama,
   I will aye be true to thee!

ALASKA
Alaska's Flag

Words by
MARIE DRAKE (1888-1963)

Music by
ELINOR DUSENBURY (c.1890-1980)

Officially adopted on 23 February 1955.
The poem "Alaska's Flag" first appeared in the October 1935 School Bulletin, published by the State's Department of Education.
Marie Drake was an employee of that department, having become Assistant Commissioner of Education in 1934.

flow'rs near - by; The gold of the ear - ly

sour - doughs dreams, The pre - cious gold of the

hills and streams; The bril - liant stars in the

north - ern sky, The "Bear," the "Dip - per," and

shin - ing high, The great North star with its

stead - y light, O'er land and sea a

be - con bright, A - LAS - KA'S FLAG to A -

- las - kans dear, The sim - ple flag of a last fron- tier.

rall. molto

8

ARIZONA
Arizona March Song

Words by
MARGARET ROWE CLIFFORD (1896-1926)*

Music by
MAURICE BLUMENTHAL (*d.*1955)†
Arr. by W. L. REED

Allegro con spirito

1. Come to this land of sun-shine To this land where life is young, Where the wide, wide world is wait-ing The songs that will now be sung. Where the

Officially adopted on 28 February 1919.
* Margaret Rowe Clifford was born in Canada.
† Year of birth unknown.
This State Song or Anthem was adopted by the Fourth State Legislature.

golden sun is flaming In-to warm, white, shin-ing day. And the sons of men are blaz-ing Their price-less right of way.

CHORUS

Sing the song that's in your hearts—— Sing—— of the great South-

west, Thank God for Ar - i - zon - a In

splen - did sun - shine dressed. For thy beau - ty and thy

grand - eur, For thy re - gal robes so sheen. We hail

thee, Ar - i - zon - a, Our— god - dess and our queen.

2. Come stand beside the rivers
   Within our valleys broad.
   Stand here with heads uncovered,
   In the presence of our God!
   While all around about us
   The brave, unconquered band,
   As guardians and landmarks
   The giant mountains stand.

   CHORUS

3. Not alone for gold and silver
   Is Arizona great.
   But with graves of heroes sleeping
   All the land is consecrate!
   O come and live beside us,
   However far ye roam.
   Come help us build up temples
   And name those temples "home".

   CHORUS

ARKANSAS
Arkansas

Words and music by
EVA WARE BARNETT (1881-1978)

1. I am think-ing tonight of the South-land, Of the home of my child-hood days, Where I

Officially adopted on 9 February 1917.

13

roamed through the woods and the mea-dows, By the mill and the brook that

plays; Where the roses are in bloom, And the sweet mag-no-lia too, Where the

jas-mine is white, And the fields are vio-let blue, There a

wel-come a-waits all her chil-dren Who have wan-dered a-far from

CHORUS

home.   Ark - an - sas, Ark - an - sas, 'Tis   a   name dear,   'Tis the

place I call "Home, Sweet Home;"   Ark - an - sas, Ark - an - sas,   I sa -

- lute   thee,   From   thy   shel - ter   no more   I'll   roam.

2. 'Tis a land full of joy and of sunshine,
   Rich in pearls and in diamonds rare,
   Full of hope, faith and love for the stranger,
   Who may pass 'neath her portals fair;
   There the rice fields are full,
   And the cotton, corn and hay,
   There the fruits of the field bloom
   In winter months and May,
   'Tis the land that I love, First of all dear,
   And to her let us all give cheer.

CHORUS

15

CALIFORNIA
I Love You, California

Words by
FRANK SILVERWOOD (1863-1924)*

Music by
ABRAHAM FRANKENSTEIN (1873-1934)

Officially adopted on 26 April 1951.

* Frank Silverwood was born in Canada.

"I Love You, California" was first introduced to the public in 1913 by Mary Garden. In 1915 it became the official song of the San Francisco and San Diego Expositions.

spring, and in the fall_____ I love your fer - tile

val - leys; your dear moun - tains I a - dore_____

_____ I love your grand old o - cean and I

love her rug-ged shore._____

CHORUS (Trio)

Where the snow crown-èd Gold - en Si - er - as

Keep their watch o'er the val - leys bloom,_____ It is there I would

be in our land by the sea, Ev - 'ry breeze bear-ing rich per - fume,_____

It is here na-ture gives of her rar - est_____ It is Home Sweet

Home to me,———— And I know when I die I shall

breathe my last sigh For my sun-ny Cal - i - forn - ia.

2. I love your redwood forests, love your fields of yellow grain.
   I love your summer breezes and I love your winter rain.
   I love you, land of flowers; land of honey, fruit and wine.
   I love you, California; you have won this heart of mine.

   CHORUS

3. I love your old gray Missions, love your vineyards stretching far.
   I love you, California, with your Golden Gate ajar.
   I love your purple sunsets, love your skies of azure blue.
   I love you, California; I just can't help loving you.

   CHORUS

4. I love you, Catalina, you are very dear to me.
   I love you, Tamalpais, and I love Yosemite.
   I love you, Land of Sunshine, Half your beauties are untold.
   I loved you in my childhood, and I'll love you when I'm old.

   CHORUS

COLORADO
Where The Columbines Grow

Words and music by
ARTHUR JOHN FYNN (1857-1930)

1. Where the snow - y peaks gleam in the moon - light, A - bove the dark for - ests of pine,

Officially adopted on 8 May 1915.

20

best, The— pi - o - neer land that we love.——————

CHORUS a tempo

'Tis the land where the col - um - bines grow,——————— O - ver look-ing the

plains far be - low,——————— While the cool sum - mer breeze in the

ev - er - green trees Soft - ly sings where the col - um - bines grow.——————

2. The bison is gone from the upland,
   The deer from the canyon has fled,
   The home of the wolf is deserted,
   The antelope moans for his dead,
   The warwhoop re-echoes no longer,
   The Indian's only a name,
   And the nymphs of the grove in their loneliness rove,
   But the columbine blooms just the same.

   CHORUS

3. Let the violet brighten the brookside,
   In sunlight of earlier spring,
   Let the clover bedeck the green meadow,
   In days when the orioles sing,
   Let the goldenrod herald the autumn;
   But, under the midsummer sky,
   In its fair Western home, may the columbine bloom
   Till our great mountain rivers run dry.

   CHORUS

CONNECTICUT
Yankee Doodle

Words and music Traditional
Arr. by W. L. REED

Allegro con spirito

Yan - kee Doo - dle went to town, Rid - ing on a po - ny,

Stuck a fea - ther in his hat, And called it ma - ca - ro - ni.

CHORUS

Yan - kee Doo - dle keep it up, Yan - kee Doo - dle dan - dy,

Officially adopted on 1 October 1978.

24

Mind　　the mus - ic　and　the step, And　with the folks　be　hand　-　y.

13

DELAWARE
Our Delaware

Words by
GEORGE HYNSON (1862-1926)

Music by
WILLIAM BROWN (1860-1917)

1. Oh the hills of dear New Cas - tle, And the smil - ing vales be - tween, When the corn is all in tas - sel, And the mead - ow lands are green; Where the cat - tle crop the clo - ver, And its breath is in the

Officially adopted on 7 April 1925.
Used by permission of the Delaware State Department, Division of Archives and Cultural Affairs.
Copyrighted. May not be reproduced in any form without written permission.

26

CHORUS **Tempo di Marcia**

air, While the sun is shin-ing o - ver Our be - lov - ed Del - a -

ware._____ Oh, our Del - a - ware! Our be - lov - ed

Del - a - ware! For the sun is shin-ing o - ver our be - love - ed Del - a -

ware, Oh! our Del - a - ware! Our be - lov - ed

27

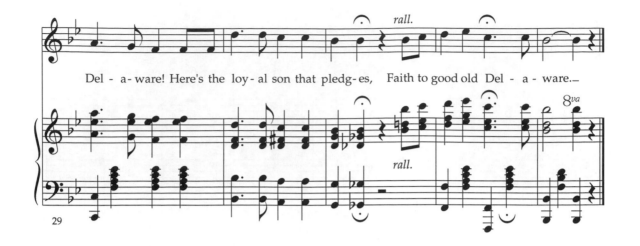

Del - a-ware! Here's the loy - al son that pledg- es, Faith to good old Del - a - ware.—

2. Where the wheat fields break and billow
   In the peaceful land of Kent,
   Where the toiler seeks his pillow
   With the blessings of content;
   Where the bloom that tints the peaches
   Cheeks of merry maidens share,
   And the woodland chorus preaches
   A rejoicing Delaware.

   CHORUS

3. Dear old Sussex visions linger
   Of the holly and the pine,
   Of Henlopens jeweled finger,
   Flashing out across the brine;
   Of the gardens and the hedges,
   And the welcome waiting there,
   For the loyal son that pledges
   Faith to good old Delaware.

   CHORUS

New Stanza authorized by the 120th General Assembly on a trial basis

   From New Castle's rolling meadows,
   Through the fair rich fields of Kent,
   To the Sussex shores hear echoes
   Of the pledge we now present:
   Liberty and Independence,
   We will guard with loyal care,
   And hold fast to freedom's presence,
   In our Home State Delaware.

   CHORUS

FLORIDA
Old Folks At Home

Words and music by
STEPHEN COLLINS FOSTER (1826-1864)*

Moderato

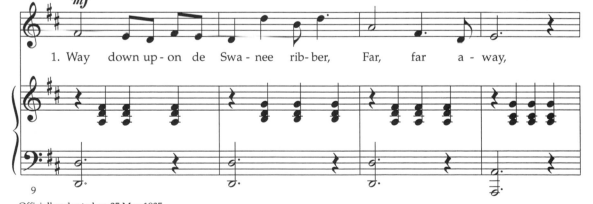

1. Way down up-on de Swa-nee rib-ber, Far, far a-way,

Officially adopted on 25 May 1935.
* Stephen Collins Foster also wrote the words and music of the State Song of Kentucky. Foster's well-known song "Old Folks at Home,"
also known as "The Swanee River," was originally published in 1851.

Dere's wha my heart is turn-ing eb-ber, Dere's wha de old folks stay.

13

All up and down de whole cre-a-tion Sad-ly I roam,

17

Still long-ing for de old plan-ta-tion, And for de old folks at home.

21

CHORUS

All de world am sad and drea-ry Eb-ry-where I roam,

25

Oh! dar-keys, how my heart grows wea - ry, Far from de old folks at home.

2. All 'round de little farm I wandered
   When I was young,
   Den many happy days I squandered,
   Many de songs I sung.
   When I was playing wid my brudder,
   Happy was I;
   Oh! take me to my kind old mudder,
   Dere let me live and die.

   CHORUS

3. One little hut among de bushes,
   One dat I love,
   Still sadly to my mem'ry rushes,
   No matter where I rove.
   When will I see de bees a humming,
   All 'round de comb?
   When will I hear de banjo tumming,
   Down in my good old home?

   CHORUS

GEORGIA
Georgia On My Mind

Words by
STUART GORRELL (*d.*1963)*

Music by
HOAGY CARMICHAEL (1903-1981)

Mel-o-dies bring mem-o-ries that lin-ger in my heart.

Make me think of Geor-gia, Why did we ev-er part?

Officially adopted on 24 April 1979.
*Year of birth unknown.
Georgia also adopted an official State Waltz, "Our Georgia," in 1951. Composed by James Burch to depict the glory of the State, this was first played at the Georgia Democratic Convention in 1950.
"Georgia On My Mind." Words by Stuart Gorrell. Music by Hoagy Carmichael. Copyright © 1930 by Peermusic Ltd. Copyright Renewed. International Copyright Secured. All Rights Reserved.

Some sweet day when blos-soms fall and all the world's a song,——

I'll go back to Geor-gia 'cause that's where I be-long.

CHORUS

Geor-gia,—— Geor-gia—— the whole day through. Just an

old sweet song keeps GEOR - GIA ON MY MIND

33

dreams I see— the road leads back to you,—

Geor-gia,— Geor-gia,— no peace I

find, Just an old sweet song keeps GEOR-GIA ON MY

1. MIND.——— 2. MIND.———

mf   rit.   mf

HAWAII
Hawaii Ponoi

Words by
KING DAVID KALAKAUA (1836-1891)

Music by
HENRY BERGER (1844-1921)

Moderato

1. Ha - wai - i po - no - i Na - na i kou mo - i
1. Ha - wai - i's own true sons, Be loy - al to your chief,

Ka - la - ni A - li - i, ke A - li - i.
Your coun - try's liege and lord, The A - li - i.

CHORUS

Ma - ku - a la - ni e Ka - me - ha - me - ha e
Fath - er a - bove us all, Ka - me - ha - me - ha e,

Title of song was officially adopted 13 June 1967.

36

Na   kau - a   e   pa - le   Me   ka   i - he.
Who guard - ed   in   the   war   With   his   i - he.

13

2. *Hawaii ponoi*
   Nana i na 'lii
   Na pua muli kou
   Na pokii.

   CHORUS

3. *Hawaii ponoi*
   E ka lahui e
   O kau hana nui
   E ui e.

   CHORUS

Translation

2. Hawaii's own true sons,
   Look to your lineal chief,
   Those chiefs of younger birth,
   Younger descent.

   CHORUS

3. Hawaii's own true sons,
   People of loyal hearts,
   Thy only duty lies-
   List and abide.

   CHORUS

IDAHO
Here We Have Idaho

Words by
ALBERT TOMPKINS (1882-1968) and
McKINLEY HELM (1896-1963)

Music by
SALLIE HUME-DOUGLAS (1872-1944)

1. You've heard of the wond-ers our land does po - ssess Its beau - ti - ful val - leys and hills._____ The ma - jes - tic for - ests where na - ture a - bounds, We love ev - ery nook___ and

Officially adopted 11 March 1931.
The music had been copyrighted under the title "Garden of Paradise" in 1915. In 1917, McKinley Helm wrote the chorus, and, later, Albert Tompkins wrote additional verses to the song.
Words used by permission of the University of Idaho.

CHORUS *f*

rill. And here we have I - da - ho,_____

_____ Win - ning her way to fame;_____

Sil - ver and gold in the sun - light blaze, And ro - mance lies

in her name;_____ Sing - ing, we're

singing of you, Ah, proudly, too, All our lives

thru, We'll go Singing, singing of you,

Singing of Idaho.

2. There's only one state in this great land of ours
   Where ideals can be realized;
   The pioneers made it so for you and me,
   A legacy we'll always prize.

   CHORUS

ILLINOIS
Illinois

Words by
CHARLES CHAMBERLIN (1841-1894)

Music by
ARCHIBALD JOHNSTON*
Arr. by NORMAN LUBOFF

1. By thy riv-ers gent-ly flowing, Il-li-nois, Il-li-nois, By thy prai-ries ver-dant grow-ing, Il-li-nois, Il-li-nois, Comes an ech-o on the breeze Rust-ling through the leaf-y trees, And its

Officially adopted 30 June 1925.
* Year of birth and year of death unknown.

41

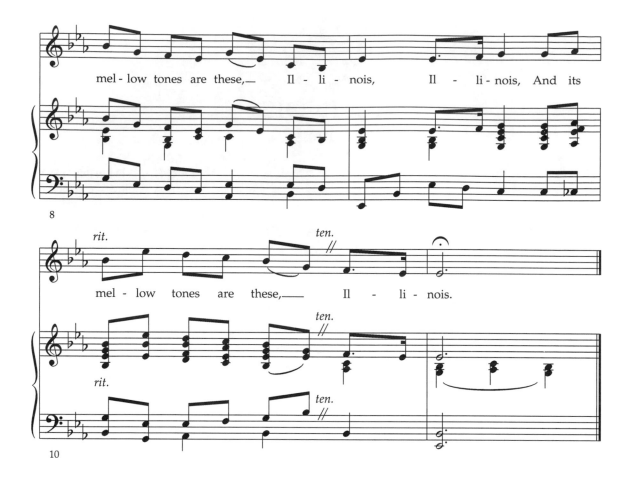

mel - low tones are these,— Il - li - nois, Il - li - nois, And its

8

rit. *ten.*

mel - low tones are these,— Il - li - nois.

10

2. Not without thy wondrous story,
Illinois, Illinois,
Can be writ the nation's glory,
Illinois, Illinois.
On the record of the years,
Abr'ham Lincoln's name appears,
Grant and Logan and our tears,
Illinois, Illinois,
Grant and Logan and our tears,
Illinois.

3. Eighteen eighteen saw your founding,
Illinois, Illinois,
And your progress is unbounding,
Illinois, Illinois.
Pioneers once cleared the land
Where great industries now stand.
World renown you do command,
Illinois, Illinois,
World renown you do command,
Illinois.

4. Let us pledge in final chorus,
Illinois, Illinois,
That in struggles still before us,
Illinois, Illinois,
To our heroes we'll be true
As their vision we pursue
In abiding love for you,
Illinois, Illinois,
In abiding love for you,
Illinois.

INDIANA
On The Banks Of The Wabash, Far Away

Words and music by
PAUL DRESSER (1857-1906)

1. Round my In-di-an-a home-stead wave the corn-fields, In the dis-tance loom the wood-lands clear and

Officially adopted 30 April 1913.

43

cool._____ Of - ten times my thoughts re - vert to scenes of

child - hood, Where I first re - ceived my les - sons, na - ture's

school._____ But one thing there is mis - sing in the

pic - ture, With - out her face it seems so in - com -

plete._____ I long to see my moth - er in the

door - way, As she stood there years a - go her boy to

CHORUS

greet!_____ Oh, the moon - light's fair to - night a - long the

Wa - bash, From the fields there comes the breath of new mown

45

hay._____ Thro' the syc - a - mores the can - dle lights are

gleam- ing, On the banks of the Wa- bash, far a - way._____

2. Many years have passed since I strolled by the river,
   Arm in arm with sweet-heart Mary by my side.
   It was there I tried to tell her that I loved her,
   It was there I begged of her to be my bride.
   Long years have passed since I strolled throu' the churchyard,
   She's sleeping there, my angel, Mary dear.
   I loved her but she thought I didn't mean it,
   Still I'd give my future were she only here.

   CHORUS

IOWA
The Song Of Iowa

Words by
SAMUEL HAWKINS MARSHALL BYERS (1838-1933)

Music Traditional*

1. You ask what land I love the best, I-o-wa, 'tis I-o-wa, The fair-est State of all the west, I-o-wa, O! I-o-wa. From yon-der Mis-sis-sip-pi's stream To where Mis-sou-ri's wa-ters gleam O!

Officially adopted 18 March 1911.
* The melody is the same as that of the State Song of Maryland.
Although inspired to write the song while in a Confederate prison in Richmond, Virginia, Samuel Byers did not do so until 1897.
Although not officially designated, the "Iowa Corn Song" by George Hamilton and popularized as early as 1912, is another Iowa song.

47

fair it is as po - et's dream, I - o-wa, in I - o-wa.

14

2. See yonder fields of tasselled corn,
   Iowa, in Iowa,
   Where Plenty fills her golden horn,
   Iowa, in Iowa.
   See how her wondrous prairies shine
   To yonder sunset's purpling line,
   O! happy land,
   O! land of mine,
   Iowa, O! Iowa.

3. And she has maids whose laughing eyes.
   Iowa, O! Iowa.
   To him who loves were Paradise,
   Iowa, O! Iowa.
   O! happiest fate that e'er was known,
   Such eyes to shine for one alone,
   To call such beauty all his own.
   Iowa, O! Iowa.

4. Go read the story of thy past.
   Iowa, O! Iowa.
   What glorious deeds, what fame thou hast!
   Iowa, O! Iowa.
   So long as time's great cycle runs,
   Or nations weep their fallen ones,
   Thou'lt not forget thy patriot sons,
   Iowa, O! Iowa.

KANSAS
Home On The Range

Words by
BREWSTER HIGLEY (1823-1911)

Music by
DAN KELLY (1843-1905)

Andante con moto

1. Oh____ give me a home Where the buff - a - lo

Officially adopted 8 April 1947.
"Home on the Range" was originally titled "My Western Home" when it was penned by Dr. Higley, a pioneeer physician in Kansas, in 1871 or 1872. In 1935, the legislature named "The Kansas March" by Duff Middleton the official State March.

roam, Where the deer and the an - te - lope play,__

Where__ sel - dom is heard a dis - cour - ag - ing

word And the skies are not cloud - y all day.__

Oh give me a land Where the bright dia - mond

Where the deer and the An - te - lope play;

Where sel - dom is heard A dis - cour - ag - ing

word, And the skies are not cloud - y all day.

2. Oh the air is so pure,
   And the zephyrs so free,
   The breezes so balmy and bright,
   That I would not exchange my home on the range
   For all of the cities bright lights.
   How often at night,
   When the heavens are bright with the light of the glittering stars,
   Have I stood there amazed and asked as I gazed
   If their glory exceeds that of ours.

   CHORUS

KENTUCKY
My Old Kentucky Home

Words and music by
STEPHEN COLLINS FOSTER (1826-1864)*

Poco Adagio

1. The sun shines bright in the old Ken-tuck-y home; 'Tis sum-mer, the peo-ple, are gay. The corn-top's ripe and the mead-ow's in the bloom, While the birds make mu-sic all the day. The

Officially adopted 19 March 1928.
*Stephen Collins Foster also wrote the words and music of the State Song of Florida.
The Kentucky state seal is reproduced with permission from the Kentucky Secretary of State.

53

young folks roll on the lit-tle cab-in floor; All mer-ry, all hap-py, and

bright. By'n by Hard Times comes a knock-ing at the door; Then, my

CHORUS

old Ken-tuck-y Home, Good-night! Weep no more, my

la-dy. Oh, weep no more to-day. We will sing one song for the

old Ken - tuck - y Home; For the old Ken - tuck - y Home, far - a - way.

23

2. They hunt no more for the possum and the coon;
   On the meadow, the hill and the shore.
   They sing no more by the glimmer of the moon;
   On the bench by the old cabin door.
   The day goes by like a shadow o'er the heart;
   With sorrow where all was delight.
   The time has come when the people have to part;
   Then, my old Kentucky home, good-night!

CHORUS

3. The head must bow and the back will have to bend;
   Wherever the people may go.
   A few more days, and the trouble all will end;
   In the field where the sugarcanes grow.
   A few more days for to tote the weary load;
   No matter 'twill never be light.
   A few more days till we totter on the road;
   Then, my old Kentucky Home, good-night!

CHORUS

LOUISIANA
Give Me Louisiana

Words and music by
DORALICE FONTANE (1906-1981)

Moderato

1. Give me Loui-si-an-a, The State where I was born, The State of snow-y cot-ton, The best I've ev-er known; A State of sweet mag-no-lias, And cre-ole mel-o-dies. Oh

Officially adopted 9 July 1970.
In 1977, the legislature also designated "You are My Sunshine" as an official State Song. The words and music are by Jimmy Davis and Charles Mitchell. In 1990, Louisiana also designated "The Gifts of Earth," music and lyrics by Francis LeBeau, as its official State Environmental Song.

give me Loui - si - an - a, The State where I was born. Oh

what sweet old mem-'ries The mos - sy old oaks bring! It

brings us the sto - ry of our E - van - ge - line. A

State of old tra - di - tion, of old plan - ta - tion days Makes

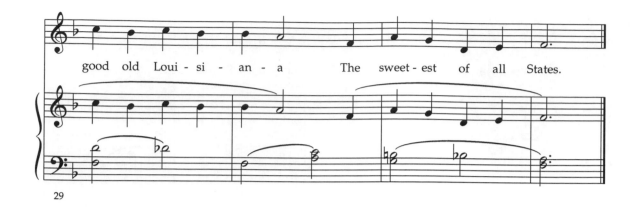

good old Loui - si - an - a   The sweet - est of all States.

29

2. Give me Louisiana,
   The State prepared to share
   That good old Southern custom,
   Hospitality so rare,
   A State of fruit and flowers,
   Of sunshine and spring showers,
   Oh give me Louisiana,
   The State where I was born.
   Its woodlands, its marshes
   Where humble trappers live,
   Its rivers, its valleys,
   A place to always give,
   A State where work is pleasure,
   With blessings in full measure
   Makes good old Louisiana
   The dearest of all States.

3. Give me Louisiana,
   Where love birds always sing,
   In shady lanes or pastures
   The cowbells softly ring.
   The softness of the sunset
   Brings peace and blissful rest.
   Oh give me Louisiana,
   The State where I was born.
   The smell of sweet clover
   Which blossoms everywhere,
   The fresh new mown hay
   Where children romp and play,
   A State of love and laughter,
   A State for all hereafter
   Makes good old Louisiana
   The grandest of all States.

MAINE
State Of Maine Song

Words and music by
ROGER VINTON SNOW (1890-1952)

Tempo di Marcia
With spirit

Grand State of Maine, proud - ly we sing To

Officially adopted 30 March 1937.

59

tell your glo - ries to the land,_____ To

shout your prais - es till the ech - oes ring._____

Should fate un - kind_____

send us to roam,_____ The

scent of the fra - grant pines, _____ the tang of the salt - y sea Will

call us home. _____

CHORUS

Oh Pine Tree State _____ Your

woods, fields _____ and hills, _____ Your

lakes   streams and   rock - bound coast Will

ev - er fill our hearts with thrills,_____ And tho' we

seek   far   and   wide,_____ Our

search_____ will   be   in   vain_____ To

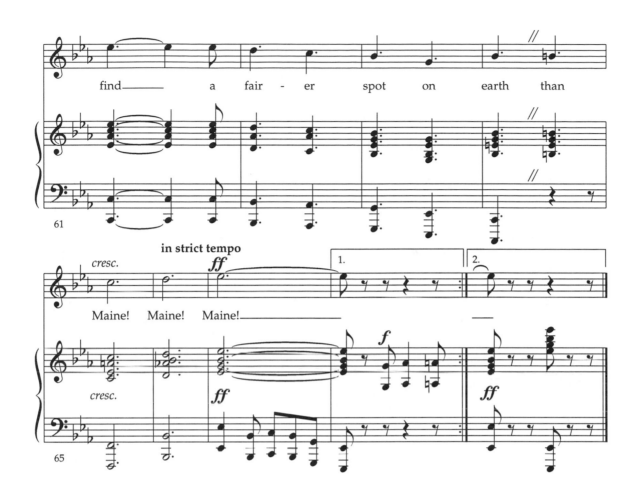

find_____ a fair - er spot on earth than

in strict tempo

Maine! Maine! Maine!_____

63

MARYLAND
Maryland, My Maryland!

Words by
JAMES RYDER RANDALL (1839-1908)

Music Traditional*

Andante

1. The des - pot's heel is on thy shore, Ma - ry- land, My

Ma - ry- land! His touch is at thy tem - ple door,

Officially adopted 26 April 1939.
* The melody is the same as that of the State Song of Iowa.
The poem, written in 1861, is sung to the tune of "Lauriger Horatius." James Randall, a Marylander who lived in the Confederacy during the Civil War, wrote the poem after Union troops went through Baltimore in 1861.

Ma - ry - land, My Ma - ry - land! A - venge the pa - tri -

ot - ic gore That fleck'd the streets of Bal - ti - more, And

be the Bat - tle - Queen of yore, Ma - ry - land, My Ma - ry - land!

2. Hark to an exiled son's appeal,
   Maryland! My Maryland!
   My mother State! to thee I kneel,
   Maryland! My Maryland!
   For life and death, for woe and weal,
   Thy peerless chivalry reveal,
   And gird thy beauteous limbs with steel,
   Maryland! My Maryland!

3.* Thou wilt not cower in the dust,
   Maryland! My Maryland!
   Thy beaming sword shall never rust,
   Maryland! My Maryland!
   Remember Carroll's sacred trust,
   Remember Howard's warlike thrust,–
   And all they slumbers with the just,
   Maryland! My Maryland!

4. Come! 'tis the red dawn of the day,
   Maryland! My Maryland!
   Come with thy panoplied array,
   Maryland! My Maryland!
   With Ringgold's spirit for the fray,
   With Watson's blood at Monterey,
   With fearless Lowe and dashing May,
   Maryland! My Maryland!

5. Come! for thy shield is bright and strong,
   Maryland! My Maryland!
   Come! for thy dalliance does thee wrong,
   Maryland! My Maryland!
   Come to thine own heroic throng,
   Stalking with Liberty along,
   And chaunt thy dauntless slogan song
   Maryland! My Maryland!

6. Dear Mother! burst the tyrant's chain,
   Maryland! My Maryland!
   Virginia should not call in vain,
   Maryland! My Maryland!
   She meets her sisters on the plain–
   "Sic Semper!" 'tis the proud refrain
   That baffles minions back again,
   Maryland! My Maryland!

7. I see the blush upon thy cheek,
   Maryland! My Maryland!
   For thou wast ever bravely meek,
   Maryland! My Maryland!
   But lo! there surges forth a shriek
   From hill to hill, from creek to creek–
   Potomac calls to Chesapeake,
   Maryland! My Maryland!

8. Thou wilt not yield the Vandal toll,
   Maryland! My Maryland!
   Thou wilt not crook to his control,
   Maryland! My Maryland!
   Better the fire upon thee toll,
   Better the blade, the shot the bowl,
   Than crucifixion of the soul,
   Maryland! My Maryland!

9. I hear the distant thunder-hum,
   Maryland! My Maryland!
   The Old Line's bugle, fife and drum,
   Maryland! My Maryland!
   She is not dead, nor deaf, nor dumb–
   Huzza! she spurns the Northern scum!
   She breathes! she burns! she'll come! she'll come!
   Maryland! My Maryland!

* The third verse is the verse usually sung.

MASSACHUSETTS
All Hail To Massachusetts

Words and music by
ARTHUR MARSH (1895-1966)

1. All hail to Mass - a - chu - setts, the land of the free and the brave! For Bun - ker Hill and Charles - town, and

Officially adopted 6 August 1981.
In 1981, Massachusetts designated also an official Commonwealth Folk Song "Massachusetts," words and music by Arlo Guthrie.
In 1989, the Commonwealth also adopted an official Patriotic Song, "Massachusetts" (Because of You Our Land is Free).

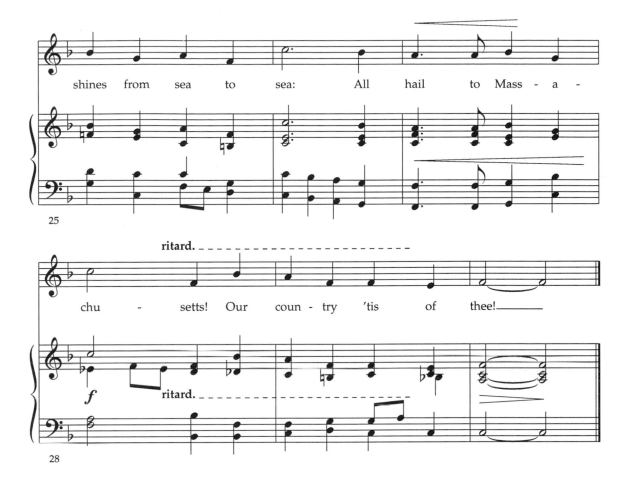

shines from sea to sea: All hail to Mass - a -

chu - setts! Our coun - try 'tis of thee!

2. All hail to grand old Bay State, the home of the bean and the cod!
Where Pilgrims found a landing and gave their thanks to God.
A land of opportunity in the good old U. S. A.
Where men live long and prosper, and people come to stay.
Don't sell her short, but learn to court her industry and stride:
All hail to grand old Bay State!
The land of Pilgrim's pride!

3. All hail to Massachusetts, renowned in the Hall of Fame!
How proudly wave her banners emblazoned with her name!
In unity and brotherhood, sons and daughters go hand in hand:
All hail to Massachusetts, there is no finer land!
It's M-A-S-S-A-C-H-U-S-E-T-T-S.
All hail to Massachusetts!
All hail! All hail! All hail!

MICHIGAN
Michigan, My Michigan

Words by
DOUGLAS MALLOCH (1877-1938)

Music by
WILLIAM OTTO MEISSNER (1880-1967)
Arr. by W. L. REED

Moderato

mf

1. A song to thee, fair State of mine, Mich-i-gan, my Mich-i-gan; But

great-er song than this is thine, Mich-i-gan, my Mich-i-gan; The

cresc.

whis-per of the for-est tree, The thun-der of the in-land sea, U-nite in

Not officially adopted.

70

one   grand sym - pho - ny Of Mich - i - gan, my Mich - i - gan.

2. I sing a State of all the best,
   Michigan, my Michigan;
   I sing a State with riches blessed,
   Michigan, my Michigan;
   Thy mines unmask a hidden store,
   But richer thy historic lore,
   More great the love thy builders bore,
   Oh, Michigan, my Michigan.

3. How fair the bosom of thy lakes,
   Michigan, my Michigan;
   What melody each river makes,
   Michigan, my Michigan;
   As to thy lakes thy rivers tend,
   Thy exiled children to thee send
   Devotion that shall never end,
   Oh, Michigan, my Michigan.

4. Thou rich in wealth that makes a State,
   Michigan, my Michigan;
   Thou great in things that make us great,
   Michigan, my Michigan;
   Our loyal voices sound thy claim –
   Upon the golden roll of Fame
   Our loyal hands shall write the same
   Of Michigan, my Michigan.

MINNESOTA
Hail! Minnesota

Words by
TRUMAN ELWELL RICKARD (1881-1948) and
ARTHUR WHEELOCK UPSON (1877-1908)

Music by
TRUMAN ELWELL RICKARD (1881-1948)
Arr. by W. L. REED

Spirited March Tempo

1. Min - ne - so - ta, Hail to thee! Hail to thee our state so dear. Thy____ light shall e - ver be A____ bea - con bright and clear. Thy____ sons and daugh - ters

Officially adopted 19 April 1945.
"Hail! Minnesota," was written in 1904-5. The music and the first verse were written by Truman Elwell Rickard.
Arthur Wheelock Upson wrote the words to the second verse. The song had first been used as the song of the University of Minnesota.

true   Will pro-claim thee near   and   far.   They will

guard thy fame and   a-dore thy name; Thou shalt be their North-ern   Star.

2. Like the stream that bends to sea,
   Like the pine that seeks the blue,
   Minnesota, still for thee
   Thy sons are strong and true.
   From thy woods and waters fair,
   From thy prairies waving far,
   At thy call they throng,
   With their shout and song,
   Hailing thee their Northern Star.

73

MISSISSIPPI
Go, Mississippi

Words and music by
WILLIAM HOUSTON DAVIS (1914-1987)

States may sing their songs of praise, With wav-ing flags and hip-hoo-rays, Let cym-bals crash and let bells ring 'Cause here's one song I'm proud to sing.

Officially adopted 17 May 1962.
The Board of Realtors of Jackson, Mississippi, set up an advisory committee to select an appropriate State Song. The committee recommended the song "Go, Mississippi."
Used by permission. Copyright Jackson Association of Realtors, Inc.
May not be reproduced in any form without written permission of the copyright owner.

GO, MISSISSIPPI, you're on the right track,
GO, MISSISSIPPI, and this is a fact,
GO, MISSISSIPPI, you'll never look back,
M-I-S-S-I-S-S-I-P-P-I.

GO, MISSISSIPPI, straight down the line,
GO, MISSISSIPPI, ev'rythings fine,
GO, MISSISSIPPI, It's your state and mine,
M-I-S-S-I-S-S-I-P-P-I.

GO, MISSISSIPPI, continue to roll,
GO, MISSISSIPPI, the top is the goal,
GO, MISSISSIPPI, you'll have and you'll hold,
M-I-S-S-I-S-S-I-P-P-I.

GO, MISSISSIPPI, get up and go,
GO, MISSISSIPPI, let the world know,
That our Mississippi is leading the show,
M-I-S-S-I-S-S-I-P-P-I.

MISSOURI
Missouri Waltz

Words by
JAMES ROYCE SHANNON (1881-1946)

Composer unknown

Hush - a - bye,   ma ba - by, slum - ber - time is com - in'

Officially adopted 22 June 1949.

soon; Rest yo' head up - on my breast while

Mom - my hums a tune; The sand - man is

call - in' where shad - ows are fall - in', While the

soft breez - es sigh as in days long gone

by.   'Way   down in   Mis - sou - ri where I

heard   this mel - o - dy,   When   I was a

lit - tle child___ on   my Mom - my's knee;   The

old folks were hum - min', Their ban - jos were strum - min' So___

79

sweet and low.

Strum, strum, strum, strum, strum,

Seems I hear those ban-jos play-in' once a-

gain, Hum, hum, hum, hum,

hum, That same old plain - tive strain.

Hear that mourn - ful mel - o - dy, It just

haunts you the whole day long, And you

wan - der in dreams back to Dix - ie, it seems, When you

hear that old - time song.

Hush - a - bye, ma ba - by, go to sleep on Mom - my's

knee, Jour - ney back to Dix - ie - land in

dreams a - gain with me; It seems like your

Mom - my is there once a - gain, And the

old folks were strum - min' that same old re -

frain. 'Way down in Mis-sou - ri where I learned this lul - la -

by, When the stars were blink - in' and the moon was climb - in'

high, Seems I hear voic - es low, as in days long a -

go Sing-in' hush - a - bye.

MONTANA
Montana

Words by
CHARLES COHAN (1884-1969)

Music by
JOSEPH HOWARD (1878-1961)

1. Tell me of that Trea - sure State, Stor - y al - ways

Officially adopted 20 February 1945.
The legislature also designated an official State Ballad, "Montana Melody," written by Carleen and LeGrande Harvey.

new,_____ Tell_____ of its beau - ties

grand And its hearts so true._____

Moun - tains of sun - set fire, The land I

love the best._____ Let me grasp the

hand of one From out the Gold - en West._____

CHORUS

Mon - ta - na, Mon - ta - na,

Glo - ry of the West._____ Of all the states from

coast to coast You're eas - i - ly the best._____ Mon -

2. Each country has its flow'r;
   Each one plays a part.
   Each bloom brings a longing hope
   To some lonely heart.
   Bitter Root to me is dear,
   Growin' in my land,
   Sing then that glorious air,
   The one I understand.

   CHORUS

NEBRASKA
Beautiful Nebraska

Words by
JIM FRAS (*b.*1925)* and
GUY MILLER (1922-1986)

Music by
JIM FRAS (*b.*1925)*

Beau-ti-ful Ne-bra-ska, peace-ful prai-rie land. Laced with ma-ny ri - vers and the hills of sand: Dark green val - leys cra-dled in the earth. Rain and sun - shine

Officially adopted 21 June 1967.
* Jim Fras was born in Russia.
Used by permission of The Willis Music Company, Cincinnati, Ohio.
May not be reproduced in any form without written permission of the copyright owner.

bring a-bun-dant birth. Beau-ti-ful Ne-bra-ska, as you look a-round,

You will find a rain-bow rea-ching to the ground: All these won-ders

by the Mast-er's hand: Beau-ti-ful Ne-bra-ska land. We are so

proud of this state where we live. There is no place that has

so much to give. Beau-ti-ful Ne-bra - ska,

as you look a-round, you will find a rain-bow rea-ching to the ground:

All these won-ders by the Mas-ter's hand. Beau-ti-ful Ne-bra - ska land.

NEVADA
Home Means Nevada

Words and music by
BERTHA RAFFETTO (1885-1952)

Tempo di Marcia

1. 'Way out in the land of the set-ting sun, Where the wind blows wild and free, There's a love-ly spot, just the

Officially adopted 6 February 1933.

92

93

Home, means the hills, Home, means the sage and the pines.

Out by the Truck-ee's sil-ver-y rills, Out where the sun al-ways

shines, There is the land that I love the best,

Fair - er than all I can see. Right in the heart of the

gold - en west Home, means Ne - va - da to me.____

35

2. Whenever the sun at the close of day
   Colors all the western sky,
   Oh, my heart returns to the desert grey
   And the mountains tow'ring high.
   Where the moon beams play in shadowed glen
   With the spotted fawn and doe
   All the livelong night until morning light
   Is the loveliest place I know.

   CHORUS

NEW HAMPSHIRE
Old New Hampshire

Words by
JOHN FRANKLIN HOLMES (1878-1955)

Music by
MAURICE HOFFMANN (1897-1982)

1. With a skill that knows no meas-ure, From the gold-en store of Fate God, in His great love and wis-dom, Made the

In 1949, the legislature declared "Old New Hampshire," to be the State Song, which was officially adopted 29 November 1977. In 1963, "New Hampshire, My New Hampshire," music by Walter P. Smith and words by Julius Richelson, was declared the second State Song.

Hamp - shire, grand and great, We will sing of Old New

Hamp - shire, Of the dear old Gran - ite State.

D.S. 𝄋

2. Builded He New Hampshire glorious
   From the borders to the sea;
   And with matchless charm and splendor
   Blessed her for eternity.
   Hers, the majesty of mountain;
   Hers, the grandeur of the lake;
   Hers, the truth as from the hillside
   Whence her crystal waters break.

   CHORUS

NEW JERSEY
I'm From New Jersey

Words and music by
JOSEPH ROCCO MASCARI (*b.*1922)
(pseudonym RED MASCARA)

I know of a state that's a per-fect play-land, With white sand-y beach-es by the sea; With fun filled moun-tains,

Not officially adopted.
The State of New Jersey does not have a State Song. Attempts to make such a designation failed. On the 20 November 1972, the General Assembly approved, a Senate bill declaring "I'm From New Jersey" the official State Song. The bill was not signed into law, however.

99

lakes and parks and folks with hos-pi-tal-i-ty. With his-

tor-ic towns where bat-tles were fought and Pres-i-dents have made their

home; It's called New Jer-sey and I toast and tout it, Wher-

ev-er I may roam. 'Cause

CHORUS Brightly (in 2)

mp - mf

a tempo

mp - mf

1. I'M FROM NEW JER - SEY and I'm
2. If you want glam - our, try At -

100

proud a - bout it. I love the Gar - den
lan - tic Cit - y, Or Wild - wood by the

State:_____ I'M FROM NEW JER - SEY and I
sea;_____ Then there is Tren - ton, Prince - ton

want to shout it, I think it's sim - ply
and Fort Mon - mouth, They all made his - to -

great._____ All of the oth - er states through -
ry._____ Each lit - tle town_____ has got that

out   the   na - tion,   May mean   a   lot   to
cer - tain   some - thing,   From High   Point   to   Cape

some;_____   But   I   would - n't   want_____   an - oth - er,
May;_____   And some place like Man - to - lo - king,

Jer - sey is like_____   no oth - er,   I'm glad   that's where   I'm
Phil - lips - burg, or_____   Ho - bo - ken,   Will steal   your heart   a -

1.
from.

2.
way._____

NEW MEXICO
O, Fair New Mexico

Words and music by
ELIZABETH GARRETT (1885-1947)

Officially adopted 14 March 1917.
In 1971, the legislature declared "Asi Es Nuevo Mejico," written by Amadeo Lucero, to be the Spanish language State Song. New Mexico also designated "Land of Enchantment - New Mexico," lyrics and music by Martin Murphy, Chick Raines and Don Cook, as its official State Ballad in 1989.

Is Nu - e - vo Me - ji - co.*   Home of the Mon - te -

zu - ma,   With fier - y heart a - glow,

State of the deeds his - tor - ic   Is Nue - vo Me - ji -

CHORUS   **Slightly faster**

co.*   O, fair New Mex - i - co,

Con 8va

*Mejico - pronounced Mĕ-hĭ-cō

104

We love, we love you so, Our hearts with pride o'er-flow,

No mat-ter where we go, O, fair New Mex - i - co,

We love, we love you so, The grand-est State to know,

New Mex - i - co.

2. Rugged and high sierras,
   With deep cañons below;
   Dotted with fertile valleys
   Is Nuevo Mejico.
   Fields full of sweet alfalfa
   Richest perfumes bestow,
   State of the apple blossoms
   Is Nuevo Mejico.

   CHORUS

3. Days that are full of heart-dreams,
   Nights when the moon hangs low;
   Beaming its benediction
   O'er Nuevo Mejico.
   Land with its bright mañana,
   Coming through weal and woe,
   State of our esperanza,
   Is Nuevo Mejico.

   CHORUS

NEW YORK
I Love New York

Words and music by
STEVE KARMEN (*b.*1937)

Officially adopted 1 July 1980.

NORTH CAROLINA
The Old North State

Words by
WILLIAM JOSEPH GASTON (1778-1844)

Music Traditional

With spirit

1. Car - o - li - na! Car - o - li - na! heav - en's bless - ings at -

tend her, While we live we will___ cher - ish, pro -

tect and de - fend her, Tho' the scorn - er may___ sneer at and

Officially adopted 18 February 1927.
Another song, "A Toast" to North Carolina, was declared the official Toast in 1957.

witlings defame her. Still our hearts swell with gladness when

CHORUS

ever we name her. Hurrah! Hur-

rah! the Old North State forever, Hur-

rah! Hurrah! the good Old North State.

2. Tho' she envies not others their merited glory,
   Say whose name stands the foremost in liberty's story,
   Tho' too true to herself e'er to crouch to oppression,
   Who can yield to just rule a more loyal submission.

   CHORUS

3. Then let all those who love us, love the land that we live in,
   As happy a region as on this side of heaven,
   Where plenty and peace, love and joy smile before us,
   Raise aloud, raise together the heart thrilling chorus.

   CHORUS

NORTH DAKOTA
North Dakota Hymn

Words by
JAMES WILLIAM FOLEY (1874-1939)

Music by
CLARENCE SIMEON PUTNAM (1859-1944)

Moderato (♩ = 72)

1. North Da - ko - ta, North Da - ko - ta, With thy prair - ies wide and free, All thy sons and daugh - thers love thee, Fair - est state from sea to

Officially adopted 15 March 1947.
In 1989, the legislature adopted "Flickertail March" by James D. Ployhar as the State March.
Courtesy of the North Dakota State Historical Society.

115

2. Hear thy loyal children singing
Songs of happiness and praise,
Far and long the echoes ringing
Through the vastness of thy ways.
North Dakota, North Dakota,
We will serve thee all our days.
North Dakota, North Dakota,
We will serve thee all our days.

3. Onward, onward, onward going,
Light of courage in thine eyes,
Sweet the winds above thee blowing,
Green thy fields and fair thy skies.
North Dakota, North Dakota,
Brave the Soul that in thee lies.
North Dakota, North Dakota,
Brave the Soul that in thee lies.

4. God of freedom, all victorious,
Give us Souls serene and strong,
Strength to make the future glorious,
Keep the echo of our song;
North Dakota, North Dakota,
In our hearts forever long.
North Dakota, North Dakota,
In our hearts forever long.

OHIO
Beautiful Ohio

Words by
BALLARD MacDONALD (1882-1935)

Music by
ROBERT KING (1862-1932)
(pseudonym MARY EARL)

Long, long a - go Some - one I know

Had a lit - tle red ca - noe, In it room for on - ly two.

Officially adopted 24 October 1969.
Curiously this 1918 waltz refers not to the State of Ohio, but to the Ohio River.

Love found its start Then in my heart, And like a
flow - er grew._____ Drift - ing with the cur - rent down a
moon - lit stream, While a - bove the Heav - ens in their
glo - ry gleam, And the stars on high_____

CHORUS

Twin - kle in the sky,———————— Seem - ing in a

Par - a - dise of love di - vine, Dream - ing of a

pair of eyes that looked in mine. Beau-ti-ful O - hi - o, in

dreams a-gain I see Vi-sions of what used to be.——————

OKLAHOMA
Oklahoma

Words by
OSCAR HAMMERSTEIN II (1895-1960)

Music by
RICHARD RODGERS (1902-1979)

Officially adopted 11 May 1953.
"Oklahoma." Lyrics by Oscar Hammerstein II. Music by Richard Rodgers. Copyright © 1943 by Williamson Music. Copyright Renewed. International Copyright Secured. All Rights Reserved.

Spin-ach and ter - may-ters! Flow-ers on the prair - ie where the June bugs

zoom, Plen'- y of air and plen'- y of room,

cresc. Plen'- y of room to swing a rope!_____ Plen'- y of

heart and plen'- y of hope._____

CHORUS *lustily*

O— k - la - hom - a, where the wind comes sweep-in' down the plain,———— And the wav - in' wheat can sure smell sweet When the wind comes right be - hind the rain.——— O—

122

k - la - hom - a, Ev - 'ry night my hon - ey lamb and I

Sit a - lone and talk and watch a hawk Mak - in'

la - zy cir - cles in the sky. We know we be -

long to the land, And the land we be - long to is

grand!_____ And when we say_____ Yeeow! A-
yip-i-o-ee ay!_____ We're on-ly say-in'
You're do-in' fine, Ok-la-hom - a! Ok-la-hom-a___
— O. K. K.___

OREGON
Oregon, My Oregon

Words by
JOHN ANDREW BUCHANAN (1863-1935)

Music by
HENRY MURTAGH (1890-1961)

1. Land of the Em-pire Buil-ders, Land of the Gold-en West;

Con - quered and held by free men, Fair-est and the best.

Officially adopted 12 February 1927.

Onward and upward ev - er, Forward and on, and on;

Hail to thee, Land of He - roes, My O - re - gon.

2. Land of the rose and sunshine,
   Land of the summer's breeze;
   Laden with health and vigor
   Fresh from the Western seas.
   Blest by the blood of martyrs,
   Land of the setting sun;
   Hail to thee, Land of Promise,
   My Oregon.

PENNSYLVANIA
Pennsylvania

Words and music by
EDDIE KHOURY (*b*.1916) and
AARON BONAWITZ (1921-1991)
(pseudonym RONNIE BONNER)

1. PENN - SYL - VA - NIA, PENN - SLY -VA - NIA. Might - y is your name, Steeped in glo - ry and tra - di - tion Ob - ject of ac -

Officially adopted 21 November 1990.

127

claim, Where brave men fought the foe of free - dom, Ty - ran - ny de -

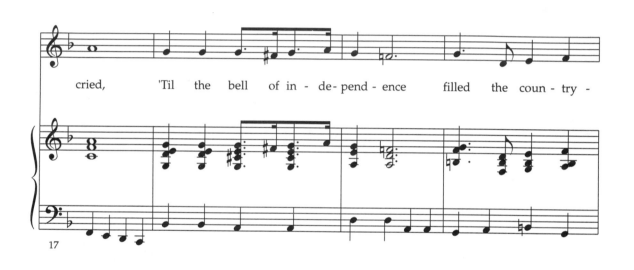

cried, 'Til the bell of in - de - pend - ence filled the coun - try -

side, PENN - SYL - VA - NIA, PENN - SYL - VA - NIA,

cresc.

May your fu - ture be filled with hon - or

poco rall.

ev - er - last - ing as your his - to - ry.

2. PENNSYLVANIA, PENNSYLVANIA,
   Blessed by God's own hand,
   Birthplace of a mighty nation,
   Keystone of the land,
   Where first our country's flag unfolded,
   Freedom to proclaim,
   May the voices of tomorrow glorify your name.
   PENNSYLVANIA, PENNSYLVANIA,
   May your future be
   Filled with honor everlasting as your history.

RHODE ISLAND
Rhode Island

Words and music by
THOMAS CLARKE BROWN (1886-1953)
Arr. by W. L. REED

March tempo

Here's to you,————— be-lov'd RHODE IS - LAND,—————

—— With your Hills and O - cean Shore.—————

Officially adopted 30 April 1946.

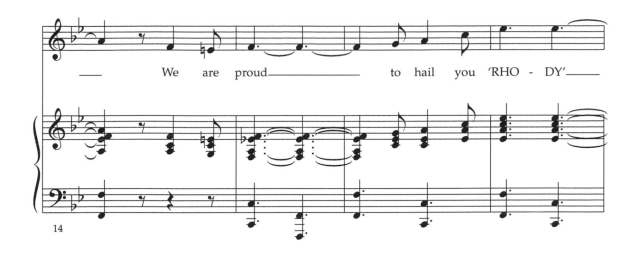

We are proud to hail you 'RHO - DY'

And your pat - ri - ots of yore.

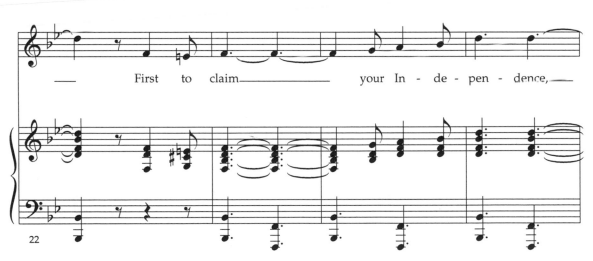

First to claim your In - de - pen - dence,

Great your her - i - tage and fame._____

The small - est State_____ in all the U - nion,____

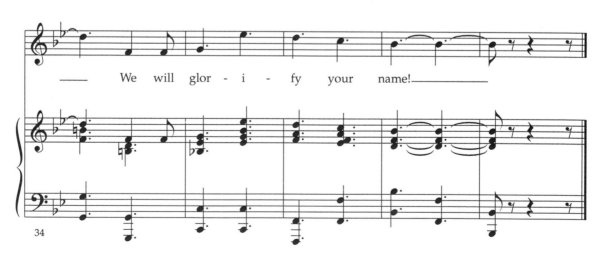

We will glor - i - fy your name!_____

SOUTH CAROLINA
Carolina

Words by
HENRY TIMROD (1828-1867)

Music by
ANNE CUSTIS BURGESS (1874-1910)

1. Call on thy chil-dren of the hill,

Wake swamp and riv-er, coast and rill,

Rouse all thy strength and all thy skill,

Officially adopted 11 February 1911.
The song "Carolina" was declared the State Song when the legislature acted on the memorial of the South Carolina Daughters of the American Revolution. "South Carolina On My Mind" was designated as a second official State Song in 1984 to promote the image of South Carolina beyond its borders.

133

Car - o - li - na! Car - o - li - na!

2. Hold up the glories of thy dead;
   Say how thy elder children bled,
   And point to Eutaw's battle-bed,
   Carolina! Carolina!

3. Thy skirts indeed the foe may part,
   Thy robe be pierced with sword and dart,
   They shall not touch thy noble heart,
   Carolina! Carolina!

4. Throw thy bold banner to the breeze!
   Front with thy ranks the threatening seas
   Like thine own proud armorial trees,
   Carolina! Carolina!

5. Girt with such wills to do and bear,
   Assured in right, and mailed in prayer,
   Thou wilt not bow thee to despair,
   Carolina! Carolina!

SOUTH DAKOTA
Hail! South Dakota

Words and music by
DEECORT HAMMITT (1893-1970)

Play in a Snappy March Time

Sing with spirit

1. Hail! South Da - ko - ta, A great state

And with her scen' - ry,

No state can com - pare.

fz

2. Come where the sun shines,
   And where life's worth your while,
   You won't be here long,
   'Till you'll wear a smile;
   No State's so healthy,
   And no folk quite so true,
   To South Dakota.
   We all welcome you.

3. Hail! South Dakota,
   The State we love the best,
   Land of our fathers,
   Builders of the west;
   Home of the Bad lands,
   And Rushmore's ageless shrine,
   Black Hills and prairies, (Hills, farms and prairies),
   Farmland and Sunshine. (Blessed with bright Sunshine).

TENNESSEE
Rocky Top

Words and music by
BOUDLEAUX BRYANT (1920-1987) and
FELICE BRYANT (*b.*1925)

1. Wish that I was on ol' Rock-y Top, down in the Ten-nes-see hills;

Ain't no smog-gy smoke on Rock-y Top, ain't no tel-e-phone bills.

Officially adopted 15 February 1982.
Tennessee has five official State Songs including "Rocky Top"; "My Homeland, Tennessee" by Nell Grayson Taylor and Roy Lamont Smith adopted in 1925; "When It's Iris Time In Tennessee" by Willa Mae Waid adopted in 1935; "My Tennessee" by Francis Hannah Tranum adopted in 1955; and "The Tennessee Waltz" by Redd Stewart and Pee Wee King adopted in 1965.
"Rocky Top" is used with permission of House of Bryant Publications. Copyright © 1967 by House of Bryant Publications.

Once I had a girl on Rock-y Top, half bear,— o-ther half
cat; Wild as a mink, but sweet as sod-a pop,

CHORUS

I still dream— a-bout that. Rock-y Top, you'll al-ways be
home sweet home— to me; Good ol' Rock-y Top,

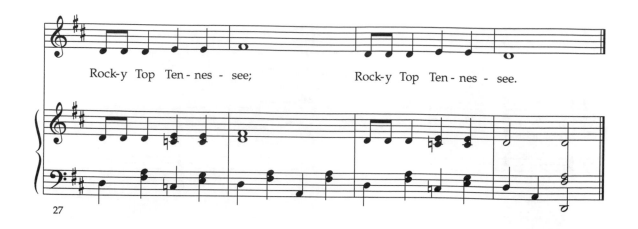

27

2. Once two strangers climbed ol' Rocky Top,
    lookin' for a moonshine still;
  Strangers ain't come down from Rocky Top;
  Reckon they never will;
  Corn won't grow at all on Rocky Top;
  Dirt's too rocky by far;
  That's why all the folks on Rocky Top
    get their corn from a jar;

  CHORUS

*3. I've had years of cramped-up city life
    Trapped like a duck in a pen;
  All I know is it's a pity life
  Can't be simple again.

  CHORUS

* begins at Bar 13

TEXAS
Texas, Our Texas

Words and music by
WILLIAM MARSH (1880-1971)*

Officially adopted 23 May 1929.
*William Marsh was born in England.
This song was chosen following contests in each senatorial district and a final contest in Dallas.
In 1933, the legislature designated a State Flower Song, "Bluebonnets," words by Julia Booth and music by Lora Crockett.
Copyright c.1925 by W. J. Marsh. Copyright renewed 1953 by William J. Marsh. Used by permission of Southern Music Company, Publisher, and Owen E. Thomas, Mary C. Hearne, Copyright owners.

141

test; O Em-pire wide and glo-rious, You stand su - preme-ly blest.

CHORUS

God bless you, Tex - as! And keep you brave and strong, That

you may grow in power and worth, Thro' - out the ag - es long.

God bless you, Tex - as! And keep you brave and strong, That

you may grow in power and worth Thro' - out the ag - es long.

2. Texas, O Texas!
   Your freeborn Single Star
   Sends out its radiance
   To nations near and far.
   Emblem of freedom!
   It sets our hearts a-glow,
   With thoughts of San Jacinto
   And glorious Alamo.

   CHORUS

3. Texas, dear Texas!
   From tyrant grip now free,
   Shines forth in splendor
   Your Star of Destiny!
   Mother of Heroes!
   We come your children true,
   Proclaiming our allegiance -
   Our Faith - Our Love for you.

   CHORUS

UTAH
Utah, We Love Thee

Words and music by
EVAN STEPHENS (1854-1930)*

1. Land of the moun-tains high, U-tah, we love thee!

Land of the sun-ny sky, U-tah, we love thee!

Far— in the glo-rious west, Thron-ed on the moun-tain's crest,

Officially adopted 21 February 1917.
*Evan Stephens was born in Wales.

144

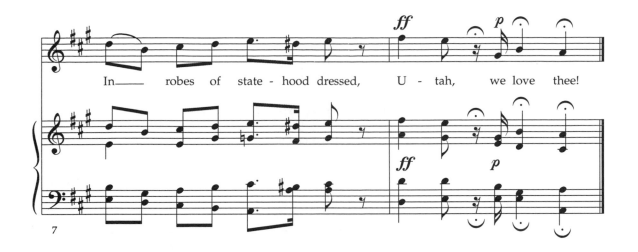

In—— robes of state - hood dressed, U - tah, we love thee!

2. Columbia's newest star,
   Utah, we love thee!
   Thy lustre shines afar,
   Utah, we love thee!
   Bright in our banner's blue,
   Among her sisters true,
   She proudly comes to view,
   Utah, we love thee!

3. Land of the Pioneers,
   Utah, we love thee!
   Grow with the coming years,
   Utah, we love thee!
   With wealth and peace in store,
   To fame and glory soar,
   God-guarded evermore,
   Utah, we love thee!

VERMONT
Hail, Vermont!

Words and music by
JOSEPHINE HOVEY PERRY (1885-1952)*

Officially adopted 13 May 1938.
* Josephine Hovey Perry was born in Canada.
"Hail, Vermont!" was selected from over 100 songs in 1938.

2. Proud of Vermont, Lovely Vermont,
   Proud of her charm and her beauty;
   Proud of her name, Proud of her fame,
   We're proud of her sense of duty;
   Proud of her past, Proud first and last,
   Proud of her lands and proud of her waters:
   Her men are true blue, her women are too,
   We're proud of her sons and proud of her daughters.

   CHORUS

VIRGINIA
Carry Me Back To Old Virginny

Words & Music by JAMES ALLEN BLAND (1854-1911)
Officially adopted on 22 February 1940

"Carry Me Back to Old Virginny" was officially adopted as Virginia's state song on 22 February 1940 and was the official state song until 1996, when it was designated "emeritus." Although that song is still sometimes used unofficially, Virginia has been conducting a contest to select a new state song, and entries have been narrowed down to semifinalists. The Commonwealth of Virginia hopes to have a new state song in the year 2000.

WASHINGTON
Washington My Home

Words and music by
HELEN DAVIS (1905-1992)
Arr. by STUART CHURCHILL

Officially adopted 19 March 1959.
In 1987, Washington also designated an official State Folk Song, "Roll On Columbia, Roll On," which was composed by Woody Guthrie.

Rest here in the sun, Filled with our laugh - ter.

Thy will be done. Wash - ing - ton my home; Where

ev - er I may roam; This is my land, my na - tive land,

Wash - ing - ton, my home. Our ver - dant for - est green, Ca -

151

ressed by sil - v'ry stream. From moun-tain peak To fields of wheat,

Wash - ing - ton, my home. There's peace you feel and un - der - stand In

this, our own be - lov - ed land. We greet the day with head held high, And

for - ward ev - er is our cry. We'll hap - py ev - er be As

peo-ple al - ways free. For you and me a des - tin - y;

1. Wash-ing-ton my home.

2. Wash-ing-ton, my home. For

you and me a des - tin-y; Wash-ing-ton, my home.

WEST VIRGINIA
The West Virginia Hills

Words by
DAVID KING (*c*.1844-1921)

Music by
HENRY EVERETT ENGLE (1849-1933)
Arr. by W. L. REED

Officially adopted 3 February 1961.
"The West Virginia Hills," was written in 1879 by The Revd. David King as a poem for his wife, Ellen King. The poem was put to music in 1885. West Virginia has adopted two other State Songs: "This Is My West Virginia" by Iris Bell and "West Virginia My Home Sweet Home" by Colonel Julian Hearne, Jr., which was designated in 1947.

stand once more with loved ones On those West Vir - gin - ia hills?

CHORUS

Oh,— the hills, beau - ti - ful hills, How I

love those West Vir - gin - ia hills! If o'er

sea o'er land I roam, Still I'll think of hap - py home, And my

friends a - mong the West Vir - gin - ia hills.

17

2. Oh, the West Virginia hills!
   Where my childhood hours were passed,
   Where I often wandered lonely,
   And the future tried to cast:
   Many are our visions bright,
   Which the future ne'er fulfills:
   But how sunny were my day-dreams
   On those West Virginia hills!

   CHORUS

3. Oh, the west Virginia hills!
   How unchang'd they seem to stand,
   With their summits pointed skyward
   To the Great Almighty's Land!
   Many changes I can see,
   Which my heart with sadness fills:
   But no changes can be noticed
   In those West Virginia hills.

   CHORUS

4. Oh, the West Virginia hills!
   I must bid you now adieu.
   In my home beyond the mountains
   I shall ever dream of you:
   In the evening time of life,
   If my Father only wills,
   I shall still behold the vision
   Of those West Virginia hills.

   CHORUS

WISCONSIN
On, Wisconsin!

Words by
Various authors

Music by
WILLIAM PURDY (1882-1918)

Officially adopted 11 July 1959.
The song was composed in 1909 by William Purdy as a football fight song. The 1959 law actually prescribes the words to be used.

WYOMING
Wyoming March Song

Words by
CHARLES EDWIN WINTER (1870-1948)

Music by
GEORGE EDWIN KNAPP (1886-1967)
Arr. by W. L. REED

Officially adopted 15 February 1955.
Copyright Margo Bean, Casper, Wyoming.
Used with permission.

159

CHORUS

breast of this great land; Where the mas- sive Rock- ies stand, There's Wy -

o - ming young and strong, the State I love! Wy -

o - ming, Wy - o - ming! Land of the sun- light clear! Wy -

o - ming, Wy - o - ming! Land that we hold so dear! Wy -

160

2. In thy flowers wild and sweet,
   Colors rare and perfumes meet;
   There's the columbine so pure, the daisy too,
   Wild the rose and red it springs,
   White the button and its rings,
   Thou art loyal for they're red and white and blue

   CHORUS

3. Where thy peaks with crowned head,
   Rising till the sky they wed,
   Sit like snow queens ruling wood and stream and plain;
   Neath thy granite bases deep,
   Neath thy bosom's broadened sweep,
   Lie the riches that have gained and brought thee fame.

   CHORUS

4. Other treasures thou dost hold,
   Men and women thou dost mould;
   True and earnest are the lives that thou dost raise,
   Strength thy children thou dost teach,
   Nature's truth thou giv'st to each,
   Free and noble are thy workings and thy ways

   CHORUS

5. In the nation's banner free
   There's one star that has for me
   A radiance pure and a splendor like the sun;
   Mine it is, Wyoming's star,
   Home it leads me near or far;
   O Wyoming! all my heart and love you've won!

   CHORUS

APPENDIX

STATE	CAPITAL	STATEHOOD	
Alabama	Montgomery	14 December 1819	22nd State
Alaska	Juneau	3 January 1959	49th State
Arizona	Phoenix	14 February 1912	48th State
Arkansas	Little Rock	15 June 1836	25th State
California	Sacramento	9 September 1850	31st State
Colorado	Denver	1 August 1876	38th State
Connecticut	Hartford	9 January 1788	5th State
Delaware	Dover	7 December 1787	1st State
Florida	Tallahassee	3 March 1845	27th State
Georgia	Atlanta	2 January 1788	4th State
Hawaii	Honolulu	21 August 1959	50th State
Idaho	Boise	3 July 1890	43rd State
Illinois	Springfield	3 December 1818	21st State
Indiana	Indianapolis	11 December 1816	19th State
Iowa	Des Moines	28 December 1846	29th State
Kansas	Topeka	29 January 1861	34th State
Kentucky	Frankfort	1 June 1792	15th State
Louisiana	Baton Rouge	30 April 1812	18th State
Maine	Augusta	15 March 1820	23rd State
Maryland	Annapolis	28 April 1788	7th State
Massachusetts	Boston	6 February 1788	6th State
Michigan	Lansing	26 January 1837	26th State
Minnesota	Saint Paul	11 May 1858	32nd State
Mississippi	Jackson	10 December 1817	20th State
Missouri	Jefferson City	10 August 1821	24th State
Montana	Helena	8 November 1889	41st State
Nebraska	Lincoln	1 March 1867	37th State
Nevada	Carson City	31 October 1864	36th State
New Hampshire	Concord	21 June 1788	9th State
New Jersey	Trenton	18 December 1787	3rd State
New Mexico	Santa Fe	6 January 1912	47th State
New York	Albany	26 July 1788	11th State
North Carolina	Raleigh	21 November 1789	12th State
North Dakota	Bismarck	2 November 1889	39th State
Ohio	Columbus	1 March 1803	17th State
Oklahoma	Oklahoma City	16 November 1907	46th State
Oregon	Salem	14 February 1859	33rd State
Pennsylvania	Harrisburg	12 December 1787	2nd State
Rhode Island	Providence	29 May 1790	13th State
South Carolina	Columbia	23 May 1788	8th State
South Dakota	Pierre	2 November 1889	40th State
Tennessee	Nashville	1 June 1796	16th State
Texas	Austin	29 December 1845	28th State
Utah	Salt Lake City	4 January 1896	45th State
Vermont	Montpelier	4 March 1791	14th State
Virginia	Richmond	25 June 1788	10th State
Washington	Olympia	11 November 1889	42nd State
West Virginia	Charleston	20 June 1863	35th State
Wisconsin	Madison	29 May 1848	30th State
Wyoming	Cheyenne	10 July 1890	44th State

COMPOSERS

BARNETT, Eva Ware (1881-1978) 13
BERGER, Henry (1844-1921) 36
BLAND, James Allen (1854-1911) 149
BLUMENTHAL, Maurice (d.1955) 9
BONAWITZ, Aaron (1921-1991) (pseudonym Ronnie Bonner) 127
BROWN, Thomas Clarke (1886-1953) 130
BROWN, William (1860-1917) 26
BRYANT, Boudleaux (1920-1987) 138
BRYANT, Felice (b.1925) 138
BURGESS, Anne Custis (1874-1910) 133
CARMICHAEL, Hoagy (1903-1981) 32
DAVIS, Helen (1905-1992) 150
DAVIS, William Houston (1914-1987) 74
DRESSER, Paul (1857-1906) 43
DUSENBURY, Elinor (c.1890-1980) 6
ENGLE, Henry Everett (1849-1933) 154
FONTANE, Doralice (1906-1981) 56
FOSTER, Stephen Collins (1826-1864) 29, 53
FRANKENSTEIN, Abraham (1873-1934) 16
FRAS, Jim (b.1925) (born in Russia) 89
FYNN, Arthur John (1857-1930) 20
GARRETT, Elizabeth (1885-1947) 103
GUSSEN, Edna Gockel (1878-1937) 4
HAMMITT, Deecort (1893-1970) 135
HOFFMANN, Maurice (1897-1982) 96
HOWARD, Joseph (1878-1961) 85
HUME-DOUGLAS, Sallie (1872-1944) 38
JOHNSTON, Archibald 41
KARMEN, Steve (b.1937) 107
KELLY, Dan (1843-1905) 49
KHOURY, Eddie (b.1916) 127
KING, Robert (1862-1932) (pseudonym Mary Earl) 117
KNAPP, George Edwin (1886-1967) 159
MARSH, Arthur (1895-1966) 67
MARSH, William (1880-1971) (born in England) 141
MASCARI, Joseph Rocco (b.1922) (pseudonym Red Mascara) 99
MEISSNER, William Otto (1880-1967) 70
MURTAGH, Henry (1890-1961) 125
PERRY, Josephine Hovey (1885-1952) (born in Canada) 146
PUTNAM, Clarence Simeon (1859-1944) 115
PURDY, William (1882-1918) 157
RAFFETTO, Bertha (1885-1952) 92
RICKARD, Truman Elwell (1881-1948) 72
RODGERS, Richard (1902-1979) 120
SNOW, Roger Vinton (1890-1952) 59
STEPHENS, Evan (1854-1930) (born in Wales) 144

LYRICISTS

BARNETT, Eva Ware (1881-1978) 13
BLAND, James Allen (1854-1911) 149
BONAWITZ, Aaron (1921-1991) (pseudonym Ronnie Bonner) 127
BROWN, Thomas Clarke (1886-1953) 130
BUCHANAN, John Andrew (1863-1935) 125
BRYANT, Boudleaux (1920-1987) 138
BRYANT, Felice (b.1925) 138
BYERS, Samuel Hawkins Marshall (1838-1933) 47
CHAMBERLIN, Charles (1841-1894) 41
CLIFFORD, Margaret Rowe (1896-1926) (born in Canada) 9
COHAN, Charles (1884-1969) 85
DAVIS, Helen (1905-1992) 150
DAVIS, William Houston (1914-1987) 74
DRAKE, Marie (1888-1963) 6
DRESSER, Paul (1857-1906) 43
FOLEY, James William (1874-1939) 115
FONTANE, Doralice (1906-1981) 56
FOSTER, Stephen Collins (1826-1864) 29, 53
FRAS, Jim (b.1925) (born in Russia) 89
FYNN, Arthur John (1857-1930) 20
GARRETT, Elizabeth (1885-1947) 103
GASTON, William Joseph (1778-1844) 112
GORRELL, Stuart (d.1963) 32
HAMMERSTEIN II, Oscar (1895-1960) 120
HAMMITT, Deecort (1893-1970) 135
HELM, McKinley (1896-1963) 38
HIGLEY, Brewster (1823-1911) 49
HOLMES, John Franklin (1878-1955) 96
HYNSON, George (1862-1926) 26
KALAKAUA, David (1836-1891) (King of Hawaii) 36
KARMEN, Steve (b.1937) 107
KEY, Francis Scott (1779-1843) 1
KHOURY, Eddie (b.1916) 127
KING, David (c.1844-1921) 154
MacDONALD, Ballard (1882-1935) 117
MALLOCH, Douglas (1877-1938) 70
MARSH, Arthur (1895-1966) 67
MARSH, William (1880-1971) (born in England) 141
MASCARI, Joseph Rocco (b.1922) (pseudonym Red Mascara) 99
MILLER, Guy (1922-1986) 89
PERRY, Josephine Hovey (1885-1952) (born in Canada) 146
RAFFETTO, Bertha (1885-1952) 92
RANDALL, James Ryder (1839-1908) 64
RICKARD, Truman Elwell (1881-1948) 72
SHANNON, James Royce (1881-1946) 77
SILVERWOOD, Frank (1863-1924) (born in Canada) 16
SNOW, Roger Vinton (1890-1952) 59
STEPHENS, Evan (1854-1930) (born in Wales) 144
TIMROD, Henry (1828-1867) 133
TOMPKINS, Albert (1882-1968) 38
TUTWILER, Julia Strudwick (1841-1916) 4
UPSON, Arthur Wheelock (1877-1908) 72
WINTER, Charles Edwin (1870-1948) 159

TITLES

Alabama 4
Alaska's Flag 6
All Hail To Massachusetts 67
Arizona March Song 9
Arkansas 13
Beautiful Nebraska 89
Beautiful Ohio 117
Carolina 133
Carry Me Back To Old Virginny 149
Georgia On My Mind 32
Give Me Louisiana 56
Go, Mississippi 74
Hail! Minnesota 72
Hail! South Dakota 135
Hail, Vermont! 146
Hawaii Ponoi 36
Here We Have Idaho 38
Home Means Nevada 92
Home On The Range 49
Illinois 41
I Love New York 107
I Love You, California 16
I'm From New Jersey 99
Maryland, My Maryland! 64
Michigan, My Michigan 70
Missouri Waltz 77
Montana 85
My Old Kentucky Home 53
North Dakota Hymn 115
O, Fair New Mexico 103
Oklahoma 120
Old Folks At Home 29
Old New Hampshire 96
Old North State, The 112
On The Banks Of The Wabash, Far Away 43
On, Wisconsin! 157
Oregon, My Oregon 125
Our Delaware 26
Pennsylvania 127
Rhode Island 130
Rocky Top 138
Song Of Iowa, The 47
Star-Spangled Banner, The 1
State Of Maine Song 59
Texas, Our Texas 141
Utah, We Love Thee 144
Washington My Home 150
West Virginia Hills, The 154
Where The Columbines Grow 20
Wyoming March Song 159
Yankee Doodle 24

About the Author

M. J. BRISTOW is an independent researcher, musician and composer. He is co-editor of *National Anthems of the World* (ninth edition, 1997).